# DAD:
## MY HERO,
## OUR JOURNEY

# DAD:
## MY HERO,
### OUR JOURNEY

 Eric R. LeFurge

iUniverse®

# DAD: MY HERO, OUR JOURNEY

*iUniverse books may be ordered through booksellers or by contacting:*

*iUniverse*
*1663 Liberty Drive*
*Bloomington, IN 47403*
*www.iuniverse.com*
*1-800-Authors (1-800-288-4677)*

*Because of the dynamic nature of the Internet, any web addresses or links contained in this book may have changed since publication and may no longer be valid. The views expressed in this work are solely those of the author and do not necessarily reflect the views of the publisher, and the publisher hereby disclaims any responsibility for them.*

*Any people depicted in stock imagery provided by Getty Images are models, and such images are being used for illustrative purposes only. Certain stock imagery © Getty Images.*

*ISBN: 978-1-5320-4408-3 (sc)*
*ISBN: 978-1-5320-4407-6 (e)*

*Library of Congress Control Number: 2018903314*

*Print information available on the last page.*

*iUniverse rev. date: 03/16/2018*

# Contents

To my father, Rusty, who passed away in 2013
after his bout with cancer

# Foreword

I asked my sister, Melissa, to write the foreword for this book. The following is what she shared.

...

Fatherhood in our family was synonymous with strength, valor, hard work, a bad temper, cussing, camping trips, tractors, and a faithful dog by your side. Our parents came from a generation older than that of our peers—one where fathers worked all day and could expect to come home to a cold beer and a nap and where mothers dutifully took care of the children, cooked, cleaned, and watched soap operas. We weren't a rich family by any means, but we lived comfortably. Dad grew up dirt-poor and always made sure we had the things he didn't when he was growing up—like yearly vacations, instruments for band class, and new clothes whenever we outgrew ours.

One of my favorite memories as a family is probably one of the most mundane. Every Friday night, we'd drive into the bigger nearby town to do our grocery shopping for the following week, but before we went shopping, we'd go out to eat. This was such a treat for us, and I looked forward to it all week. We never went to extravagant places—Ponderosa Steakhouse was our favorite until it went out of business—but I still loved it. On the way home, Dad would almost always pull into one particular convenience store's parking lot, and he'd let us get either a candy bar or a soda, while Mom waited patiently in the car. Eric would usually get a soda, and I'd almost always get candy.

In our family, it's safe to say I was the prodigal son—well, daughter. I moved out and returned home almost more times than I can count. I'd get a lofty dream in my head, save up a large sum of money, pack up my truck, and move to a faraway land. Mom would cry, and Dad would tell me that he hoped I found myself out there. Just like the parable, things would not go as planned; I'd party too hard, run out of money, and return home, willing to declare myself no longer worthy and ready for them to treat me as a hired servant to earn my keep. Instead of chastising me, both parents would welcome me home with open arms, no questions asked. I was a vegetarian at the time, so they killed no fattened calves on my behalf.

Dad was the first person who explained death and dying to me. When I was about four, we were watching a television show (that a four-year-old probably shouldn't have watched), and in it, a woman died from a car accident. When I asked him what happened, he explained that the woman died—she lost her life. Death is a pretty abstract concept for a child that young, and I just didn't get it. In a very calm and patient manner, he explained that death happens when your heart stops beating. I still don't think I really understood it until our pet guinea pig died about a year and a half later. Dad dug a hole in the side yard, we said our goodbyes, and we buried her in Eric's Transformers shoebox. I was with Dad when his heart stopped beating, and I still have a hard time wrapping my head around his death.

This book is dedicated to all the dads who loved, who were tough, and who loved tough. Dads who showed their dedication to their family through tireless hard work, who sometimes showed their anger more than their tenderness, and who felt more deeply than they even had the words to express. Dads who pushed you to face what you feared the worst but reminded you to always have faith in the best. More important, this is dedicated to our dad—the one who taught us to feel proud of our accomplishments, who forgave us for our failures, and who told us we could do anything we put our minds to.

Rusty's daughter,
Melissa LeFurge

# Chapter 1

# THE INTRODUCTION

I walked back into my classroom on the morning of April 29, 2013. I found it hard to believe that I had been gone for two weeks. I sensed that I would not have an easy day. Thinking back on the last couple of weeks, I pondered how my world had gotten turned upside down. That chilling phone call I had received two weeks before still rang in the back of my mind.

Toward the end of the day, my phone flashed that someone had left me a voice mail. As I looked at the number, my heart felt as if it fell into my stomach. Tears started flooding from my eyes. My mom had left the voice mail. After dismissal, I hurried back to my classroom to call home. My mom had just enough strength to tell me that my dad wouldn't make it and would probably leave us that day or the next day.

Of course, as you can imagine, news like this doesn't make you want to shout with joy. I contacted my principal shortly after I hung up the phone. She came down and wanted to know what I needed to share with her. After I explained the situation to her, I had a complete meltdown. She asked what she could do to help, and I let her know I would need at least the rest of the week to go be with my family. After she left, my wife came in to see what was going on. I explained to her what my mom had told me. I could see the disbelief in her expression. Realizing the gravity of the situation, I left work as soon as I could. I needed to get home in order to pack for the long expedition.

As I packed, I began to think about all the times my family gets together. We don't do it very often, as my sister, Melissa, lives in California and I live in North Carolina. My sister had just flown in that morning and had already made it to our parents' house. Sitting in my bedroom, I prepared materials my substitute would teach in my absence, and at about eight at night, I received a call from Melissa. I felt a huge lump in my throat as I answered the call. Nobody ever wants to go through this moment, but it's something that we can't avoid in life.

"Hello?" I answered. I found it difficult to hear my sister through all the emotional noises in the background.

"Dad just died," Melissa informed me.

"When did it happen?" I asked my sister.

"Just now," she replied.

"Tell Mom I will be there tomorrow. I will book a flight to Michigan and let you know when I'm arriving in Detroit," I said. "I am packing right now."

"Okay, I'll let her know," answered Melissa.

I didn't say anything about feeling angry at myself, but I did, because I was the only immediate family member who hadn't been there at the moment Dad died. I thought I let my family down because I should have been there with them. But I found it somewhat comforting that some of my relatives and my parents' pastor were there when it happened.

At that point, I thought, *Why on earth did God let this happen? It's not fair that this happened. Dad had so many plans that he wanted to fulfill after he retired this summer. It's just not fair!*

My family was no stranger to cancer. My aunt had cancer about twenty years ago. The doctors caught it quick enough that it didn't have a chance to spread to vital organs. It's a whole other ball game with relatives than it is with your parent. With every item I packed, I became angrier and angrier. As tears continued to streak down my face, I just couldn't help but think about how lucky we had thought we were that God would perform this miracle and fully heal Dad. We had thought we would have a huge celebration—one that the world would know. Instead, it felt as if we were on the losing end of a Hail Mary pass with no time remaining in the game.

As emotions kept swirling in my mind, my thoughts turned to my mom. *How can you lose someone you've been married to for forty-plus years?* I tried to grasp that. *What will happen to Mom now? How will she react?* All these questions came to mind. I couldn't fathom the idea that Dad was really gone—well, not really gone but waiting for us in heaven. I didn't know how I felt about that. Knowing that Dad was no longer in pain but also no longer here in the physical sense really played with my emotions. Part of me rejoiced, and the other part of me remained very angry that it happened this way. What about tractors? Motorcycles? Traveling? Grandkids? He was supposed to take the path to happiness, but not anymore. This was supposed to be the greatest time of our lives, but now it was completely washed out. Why was life so unfair? What about all those adventures he'd planned? He had no notice given.

I have spent a lot of nights thinking, *What if …?* I have spent many nights crying myself to sleep. I have spent many nights going to sleep angry. I looked for any kind of solace. I looked for answers, but nobody seemed to have any. I have a picture of my dad in the front room of my house, where I spend the most time. In it, my dad sits on his Harley-Davidson, looking like a member of a motorcycle club. When I look at that picture, I smile because he really enjoyed riding that motorcycle. I also find myself saddened because I will never get to see him ride that motorcycle again. In the eyes of mere mortals, we could view this as a tragedy. In the eyes of heaven, we look at this as a celebration.

My dad was the type of person who expected excellence. However, he showed his approval and disapproval in different ways. He always quickly rewarded my sister and me when we did something in excellence. In some ways, he liked living his dreams through us. No dream was more important than the different things we did.

Chapter 2

# SCOUTING – THE SCHOOL YEARS

When I was young, Dad had me participate in the scouts. Dad had taken part in scouting as a young boy but never got the chance to go very far. I found those some great and some difficult times. When I raced against his car that he built as a child in the pinewood derby, I had one of those moments when you understand how a father can connect with his son.

One time, sitting at the kitchen table, Dad helped me through the Cub Scout book so I could earn arrowheads for each level. But I just didn't want to do any more for that evening. Normally, I felt self-motivated to complete activities, but in that instance, I didn't want to go any further. In frustration with my lack of enthusiasm, Dad took the book and threw it as hard as he could across the kitchen. I can remember feeling much resentment as I thought of continuing my path in scouting. My mom, who always seemed to be the voice of reason, tried to calm Dad down enough to stop shouting at my mom or me. After he calmed down, he walked over and picked up the book. I could see in his eyes that he felt sorry, but he never said anything about it. I think that was the mental aspect of our relationship. We had times where we didn't apologize for things we did to each other, but we knew deep down in our hearts that we truly forgave each other.

My trip through Cub Scouts and then Boy Scouts seemed to have the same results in everything we did. One time, our Boy Scouts troop went to Philmont for a weeklong backpacking excursion through the Rocky Mountains of New Mexico. The excursion started with a bus trip from

Michigan. That summer, major flooding happened over the Great Plains, and the train trip we originally planned had to change.

The first day, Dad had me in tears. I had planned to tent with another scout, whereas Dad thought I would tent with him. We had a big argument about tenting arrangements, and I finally had to walk away before the conversation turned very ugly. That wasn't the worst moment. About three days into our trip, a member of my group started to have difficulties keeping up with the group. My dad, as the expert backpacker, decided to hike with him. We went ahead and moved forward, reaching our destination.

About forty-five minutes later, Dad and the camper arrived, and Dad immediately went off about being left to help the camper by himself. Needless to say, the way he showed his feelings downright embarrassed me. I understood how he felt, but I didn't think it appropriate to let the whole campsite know. I think that was the turning point of our trip. Dad seemed more relaxed and enjoyed the rest of our trip after that. He listened more and allowed me to make more decisions about how we should do things.

He told me he felt especially proud of one activity on the trip. At one of the campsites where we stayed, our troop found a rock wall that scaled up about fifty feet. When my turn came, I scampered up the wall the fastest. Shortly after the activity, Dad pulled me aside and told me how proud of me he felt for climbing the wall the fastest. Later, in rummaging through some of my old things that my mom saved for me, I found a picture of our scout troop taken at the base camp. I found it sad to look at that photo and realize the two adults who chaperoned our trip were both gone.

Dad loved the outdoors. I think that's why I have a difficult time camping and hiking; they bring back wonderful memories of a time when Dad and I connected. My son, Andrew, is now involved in scouting. He loves to go camping. Every time I put up the tent for Andrew, I think of Dad and the memories that we made and I can think about for the rest of my life.

Chapter 3

# THE CALL

On my way back home from Wilmington on a sunny Wednesday afternoon, I had to make a forty-five-minute drive to purchase some items for my classroom. The school year would start in a couple of weeks, and I wanted to make sure I had everything ready for school orientation. About twenty minutes away from home, I received a call from Mom. It was a little odd for her to call me during the week, because we usually Skyped on Sundays. As I answered the call, something in my mind told me to brace myself for the unexpected.

"Hello?" I answered.

"Hi," said Mom. "Dad is in the hospital. I took him to the emergency room, and they are taking him down to Ann Arbor for testing. His calcium and potassium levels are way off."

Too stunned for words, I didn't know how to answer. Perhaps I should have pulled off the road. Maybe I should have asked Mom to call back. It seemed like an eternity before I could gather any words I was trying to get out. "Okay. Please keep me posted on what happens," I finally choked out.

That had been the worst summer I had had in a long time. I had stepped down as a soccer coach in April for personal reasons. During that summer, while I worked at a summer camp program, my left thumb got caught in someone's belt buckle. The result? A partially torn UCL in my left thumb. I would have that thumb immobile for the next ten weeks. The doctors told me it was so bad that I might need surgery on it. I had hours of therapy just so I could stand the pain. I didn't know if I could stand any worse news.

Two Fridays before our school year would begin, Mom called me late in the evening. I had just arrived home from setting up my classroom and felt terribly exhausted.

"Hello?" I answered.

"Hi," Mom replied. "I have some bad news. Dad has cancer."

I could feel Mom's emotions through the phone. I felt as if someone had just pushed me off a bridge. My heart fell into the pit of my stomach. I could feel tears starting to flood my eyes.

Mom continued, "He has a lump in his lung and three spots on his brain, and his liver is spotted with cancer. He has stage 4 lung cancer. They are going to start chemotherapy soon."

I didn't know how to react to this news. I had a whirl of emotions traveling through my mind. I had just lost my grandpa a year before that. Now, I had the reality that I could lose Dad as well.

"Do you want me to come up there?" I asked.

"No, I will just keep you informed," Mom replied.

A few moments later, Mom changed her mind. She knew that school would begin soon, and she didn't want to interfere with that. But I knew that family was more important than work. My sister, Melissa, was flying in from California to be with my parents. I wouldn't let anything stop me from going to see Dad too. I called my principal and informed her that I would need a week to spend with my family. I told her that I would try to get as much done in my classroom before my flight left later that Saturday afternoon.

I woke up extra early on Saturday morning so I could get as much done in my classroom as possible. I had spent the previous night packing my suitcase and placing it in the car so I could just drive to the airport from work and not have to worry about going back home. I couldn't tell you one thing that I remember putting up in my classroom, or anything I did to prepare for parent orientation. I couldn't tell you how I got to the airport, or anything about arriving in Detroit at a very late hour. All I can remember is praying the entire way from Jacksonville to Detroit. I remember my cousins Chipp and Suzanne picked me up at Metro Airport and drove me to St. Joseph's Hospital in Ann Arbor.

I found Mom waiting at the door to let me in. I thanked my cousins and went to give Mom a hug. I could feel tears welling up in my eyes as

I felt a sense of relief that I had made it home. I also had a sense that this would be one of the most difficult times in my life.

Then, Mom walked me up to Dad's hospital room. I could feel a river of tears flowing from my eyes when I looked at Dad. I found it a bit uncomfortable because Dad wasn't his normal self. It seemed as if he was hallucinating and didn't recognize me right away. Walking up to Dad, I took out a picture of a dinosaur that Andrew had drawn for him. Mom went over to the board and hung it up for Dad to see.

It was probably around midnight by the time Mom and I left for home. I still couldn't understand how this was happening. Only a few months before, Dad had looked healthy on our visit to Michigan. Dad looked so happy playing with Andrew and Elizabeth. He didn't exhibit any signs of cancer. He walked and talked as if nothing bothered him. That had not been the same man who now lay in a hospital bed with his life on the line.

That week, I called several of my friends to come visit with me and Dad. Dad had several days of family and friends stopping by and supporting him. I had some of my friends from the University Christian Fellowship stop by to pray for him. I felt better knowing that he was not going into this fight alone. But it was a rough week for my family and me.

A few days before I headed back home, the doctor came in to Dad's room to speak with us. We all braced ourselves to hear the information that would, ultimately, change our lives forever. I prayed that we would receive good news and that Dad would be okay. I don't know if I didn't hear him correctly the first time, but I saw the look on his face didn't exude the best news. When he informed us that Dad had two to eight months left, it devastated all of us. I had to step outside the room to gather my thoughts.

As I sat out in the hall, Dad's sisters were on their way to visit him. They saw me out in the hall, with tears streaking down my face. They asked me what was going on, and I informed them Dad didn't have much longer, maybe eight months tops. They tried to console me, but seeing as how I saw them once every few years, they didn't provide any comfort. In fact, I found myself feeling angry that it took something like this to bring us together. As far as I was concerned, they were total strangers who just popped in for a quick visit.

On my last day, the doctors decided to move Dad to a different facility. My friend Jeremy was picking me up to take me to the airport later, and

I wanted to spend as much time with Dad and Mom as possible. Melissa had left earlier in the week. As soon as Dad got comfortable, I took the time to say goodbye. Mom walked me to the facility entrance, and I asked her to keep me updated on how Dad was doing before I walked out to get into Jeremy's car.

I've known Jeremy for almost thirty years. We've gone through so much together over the years that I consider him part of my family. In the car, we made small talk about sports, jobs, and how I felt about Dad. As he pulled over to drop me off, I thanked him for the ride and prepared myself for the flight back home. As I sat waiting to board the plane, I couldn't help but think that part of me was staying behind. I felt grateful for the chance to be with Dad, and I didn't want to leave. However, I knew that I couldn't stay, and in the back of my mind, I wasn't sure I wanted to stay at that point either. As I boarded the plane, I felt emotionally exhausted.

When my plane landed back in Jacksonville, I couldn't help but think about school starting next week. Could I recover in time? Should my students know about what I was going through? What would happen to me in the worst possible situation? Quickly, I would answer all those questions.

# Chapter 4

# *SUMMERTIME FUN*

Every summer, Dad would take some vacation time, and we would travel around Michigan. Our family owned a Chevy Blazer and a pop-up camper. I was so glad we didn't have to stay in a tent. Each year, Dad and I would wash the Blazer and the pop-up camper to make them clean and ready for use. I would always help Dad back up the Blazer to hook up the camper because I guess I gave much better directions than any other family member.

Whenever we would take a long road trip, I was always the navigator. I became a great navigator because I could read maps and symbols. When Dad asked me a question, I would pick up the big map book of Michigan counties and let him know where we were and how to get to our destination. I enjoyed informing Dad of our location, and in the process, learned a lot about maps and Michigan's geography.

I think my favorite trip was our trip around Michigan's Upper Peninsula. We saw some amazing places on that trip. We started at Sault Ste. Marie, where we took a tour of the Soo Locks, the waterway that connects Lake Superior to Lake Huron. Lake Superior is at a higher level than Lake Huron, and the Locks allow ships to be raised or lowered to the proper level to move into the other lake.

I think Dad most enjoyed touring Whitefish Point. We toured this lighthouse that shines out into Lake Superior to signal to ships that they are safe. Located in Paradise, Michigan, that place is anything but paradise. Many of the ships that have sunk in Lake Superior have done so around this area. Dad loved doing anything outdoors. I think that's why he loved taking us on so many journeys during the summer.

We managed to tour the entire Upper Peninsula in one summer. I'm not sure how many times I told Dad thanks for that trip. As I became older, I knew I didn't do it enough. A man sacrificing his job in the summer to take his family on a vacation means more to me now, especially since he is gone. Sometimes I look at our vacation pictures and think, *We had such a great time as a family. We were so happy being together, doing something we loved.* I truly miss those days.

# Chapter 5

# ROUGH FIRST DAY

As I walked out to my car after my plane landed in Jacksonville, I couldn't help but wonder how I would react when I walked through the door at my home. I sat in my car a little bit to gather my thoughts so I could make the twenty-minute drive home.

As I pulled into my driveway, I knew that I would have to go into work the next day to try to get ready for the first day of school on Monday. Inside, I received hugs from my wife and kids, but unfortunately, they did little to console me. Those people who tell you that they understand don't understand unless they have gone through the process themselves as well.

I didn't sleep well the night I returned. I doubt I even got two hours of sleep that night. I had millions of things rotating through my mind. In fact, I felt a bit guilty I had to leave Mom by herself to take care of Dad. I felt a little better when I thought my aunts, Karen and Phyllis, could help keep her company. But so many what-ifs kept bothering me. I knew that I would have to try to make the best of what had become the cloud over my life.

I went into work Sunday afternoon, hoping to complete some work; however, what I found was a different place to dwell on what might or might not happen. I did get some work done while I pondered my family's future. I really appreciated the hard work other staff members had done during the week to meet and greet my students and their parents during orientation. And I couldn't help feeling a little guilty about not giving that positive first contact to my future students. I knew that I would have a heavy burden on me the next day—the first day of school. I taped nametags onto the desks where my students would sit and took a deep breath and stepped back. When I looked around the room, it just seemed meaningless for me to be there.

A few teachers stopped by to ask me how I was doing. I told them that I was doing as well as I could. I felt terrified to let them know how I really felt because I'm not one who shows sorrow in public. I got that trait from Dad. Very rarely did Dad show sorrow around my sister and me. In fact, I only remember seeing Dad cry when we went to the cemetery and he changed flowers on his mother's grave. I never got a chance to meet my grandma, and Dad didn't talk a lot about her.

As I finished up for the day, I still had a lot I needed to accomplish. Someone had put all my posters had been put up. I needed to place important documents that students' parents had to fill out on the desks. I needed to put away supplies that students had brought in during orientation. I needed to finish bulletin boards inside the classroom. Physically, I was there. Mentally and emotionally, I was still back in that hospital room, thinking, hoping, and praying that this was a bad dream. I hoped that someone would pinch me, and I would awaken to smiles, laughs, and celebrations that there was nothing wrong with my family.

As I locked my classroom door and headed out of the building, I didn't know how I would get through the first week of school. I wanted to feel excited about the new students I would teach and mentor, but my heart told me otherwise. I had a choice to make: soldier on and continue with my life, or stop everything and hope it would all turn out okay. Knowing Dad, I realized he would want me to continue. And I did.

Chapter 6

# THE BARN RAISING

I woke up in the summer of 1992, knowing that I would be very busy. Working at the local grocery store and helping Dad build our pole barn, I knew I wouldn't have a lot of time for fun. Dad needed all the help he could get.

Dad went down to the neighbor's house to borrow a tractor we would use to dig holes for the barn's posts. The previous week, trucks had delivered tons of sand as our barn's base. A site worker had already approved the barn's construction, so there was no stopping the progress. Much of the materials had already been delivered. It really excited me to build this barn, but only in the sense I would have much less grass to mow.

It was my job to run the tractor, and Dad would run the auger. However fast the tractor ran, it would spin the auger just as fast. I was also in charge of how far up and down the auger would drill. I remember watching Dad align the auger to make sure it drilled holes straight. Dad had had back problems a lot over the past twenty years, and I couldn't help thinking, *That has to cause an incredible amount of stress on Dad's back.*

After each hole was complete, I would pull up the auger and maneuver the tractor to the next posthole. The fact that I am not the tallest person in the world caused a problem. In fact, I had to lift myself off the tractor seat to reach the pedal to stop and start the auger. I can recall a few times, I got some dirty looks when my foot would slip off the pedal while trying to raise and lower the auger. I'll admit that it was probably not the best job for me. Being very thin, I knew I had no way to control where the auger went into the ground.

After we drilled all the holes, we placed, I would guess, fifteen- to twenty-foot posts into the holes. We dumped a bag of concrete into each hole. Dad had the level, so we knew when we had each pole vertically straight. After the concrete, we would place water into each hole. After that, we would fill the rest of each hole with the dirt leftover from drilling the holes. Apparently, I was naïve to think that this would be the most difficult part of constructing the barn.

After we filled all the posts, we now faced the task to put up the barn's skeleton. I don't remember working on this part of the barn very often. I guess that Dad didn't need too much help with this part. Nor do I remember the trestles being part of the barn I helped with. I remember several people Dad invited out to help with this project. I guess Dad didn't want me involved in this procedure. Maybe it was his way of telling me, "This is too dangerous for you to be involved in." I think Dad felt seriously concerned for my safety. I never asked him why he didn't need me for this task, but I knew that I had a ton of work ahead of me.

After the roof went up, Dad and I faced the challenge of putting aluminum siding on the barn. I thought this would be easy, but I regretted that thought when I smashed my thumb with a hammer as I hit the first nail into the metal siding. This would not be easy. After smashing my thumb putting up the siding for the first time, Dad let me know that he didn't want big dents in the siding. So, if I couldn't hit the nail as hard as I could, how would I get through this? Well, I guessed I would just have to be careful.

After a while, I finally got the hang of it. The only trouble I now had came when I had to drive a nail into the overlap. In case you don't know, I had to drive it through two sheets of siding. My thumb suffered on through the pain of hitting it every time I tried to drive the nail into the siding and beam. It surprised me that I didn't break my thumb into several pieces. I was relieved when I finished that task.

Here, I spent my entire summer putting up a barn with Dad, and I couldn't feel prouder of our accomplishment. I never did get a chance to marvel in amazement with Dad, but it was one of the greatest moments of our lives. Here, we had taken three months and had built this magnificent structure that would become an important part of our lives.

# Chapter 7

# *PLOWING AHEAD*

I always feel nervous on the first day of school. It doesn't matter who the students are or what school I am at. I was very jittery on that first day in August 2012. That was the first time I had met any of my students or their parents. As the bell rang and I prepared to greet my students, I felt a lump in my throat and a pain in my stomach. As the students began to enter, I greeted each child and each parent who came into the room the first time I met everyone. Many of the children were present on orientation night but obviously didn't get to meet me then.

As class began, I introduced myself and went over the expectations that I had for our class. We discussed classroom rules, school procedures, homework, and several other first-day materials. As I gathered my class on the carpet, I proceeded to inform them about the thumb I had injured during the summer. I explained to them that I had torn my UCL in my thumb, getting it caught in the belt buckle of a student whom I was playing a game with. I let them know that it would stay in the brace for another few weeks and that I might find it difficult to complete two-handed tasks.

I took a deep breath and said to myself, *Should I let these kids know what is really going on that will ultimately consume most of my mental energy during the school year?*

I took another deep breath and proceeded, telling them why I was unable to attend orientation night. As I began my story, I could feel tears welling up in my eyes. I took several deeper breaths and continued. This was the first time that cancer had affected my immediate family, and I didn't know how to share my family's story. As I looked at the children, I could see that they listened carefully and seemed to understand the gravity of the situation.

I had twenty-four pairs of eyes staring straight at me, all about as wide-open as an owl's eyes. I became terrified by all that attention. I told them that we believed that Dad would be all right and that, hopefully, he would visit sometime during the school year. By the end of my talk, I could feel sweat pouring off me. My throat was as dry as a bone. My mind wasn't anywhere near what it should have been for the first day of school.

Luckily, the first day of school provides a great opportunity to incorporate activities to get to know students better. It's a great day to see how much information the students have retained over the summer. The teacher merely facilitates such activities. That day, we completed a scavenger-hunt sheet as a get-to-know-you-better activity. We took time to go over basic addition and subtraction facts to see how much work we would need in math. Also, students created goals that they wanted to achieve by the end of the school year. I think a couple of expectations saved me from having a total meltdown that day. My principal at the time wanted us to feed our students lunch and get them home on the correct bus at the end of the day. With all the hustle and bustle of the first day of school, I merely put my family aside for the time being so I could concentrate on getting to know my class.

At the end of the day, I walked back into my empty classroom, looked around, and exhaled a large sigh. I had made it to the end of the first day of school. I didn't know what to feel at that moment. So I sat down at my desk and put my head against my hands. I felt tired. I was dirty. I couldn't believe that this was happening. Three weeks before, my family was fine. Now, my world felt as if it was in shambles. And this was only the first day of 180 days of school. If I felt this way now, I had a terrible year in store, not only for me but also for the students. Students don't want a teacher who doesn't focus on learning. I briefly considered asking for some time off, but I knew that wasn't possible. I needed my income to help support my family. I couldn't take any days off over the first few weeks and jeopardize my students' school year. And I couldn't just stay home and have Mom be the only person taking care of Dad. Only time would determine what I needed to do.

I had gotten through my first day, thanks to the power of God, but I had to think about the unthinkable. Sometimes, it helps to play out the worst-case scenario. After I arrived home, I thought about the worst thing that could happen—yeah, probably not the smartest move I could make. I felt tears welling up again. Then, I began to think about all the great times Dad and I had had together. This would get me through until Christmas. The thought even crossed my mind that Dad might be cancer-free when we would get to see him over Christmas break. I tried to think optimistically, but in the back of my mind, I knew I couldn't easily navigate this road.

# Chapter 8

# THE CAR BOND

For as long as I can remember, Dad always loved cars. I wasn't much in the car department. I guess it really didn't appeal to me. However, when it came time to get me a car, I knew that a new car was unaffordable for my parents. This meant that I had to get used to a less-than-tolerable car. Mom had a friend who was willing to give us a car, a 1981 Plymouth Turismo, if I wanted to take the time to basically rebuild it from the ground up. It didn't sound like a lot of fun to me, but I agreed because I knew that I couldn't get anything better at that moment. Dad thought it would be a lot of fun to put this car together.

When we got the car home, I could see that this car would need a lot of work. The body was rusted out in a few places. We would have to rebuild and put in an entirely new engine. I would have to replace the tires. It would need a new coat of paint. I could see that my education in cars would grow with each day we worked on the car. As Dad peered over the extent of the needed work, he figured that he would also need a couple of similar cars to help rebuild this one in front of us.

As we began taking the car apart, I didn't realize how much detail was involved in just getting some of the parts off. The two main things that we would need to accomplish were to rebuild the engine and repair the car's body. As we started to rebuild the engine, I had little knowledge of what was actually going on. I could feel Dad's frustration as I kept giving him the incorrect tool. I learned a lot about the different tools we used. As we continued to work on the car, we had some bumps along the way.

We didn't always see eye to eye, but we could tell that this process made us closer than we had been for a while.

I think I felt the most excited when we finally had the engine rebuilt and dropped it into the car. Dad had gotten an engine lift to help hold it while we moved it into place. This was the moment of truth. Would this engine be good enough to get me from point A to point B? As we put the key into the ignition, we felt excited. Dad and I hoped we wouldn't need to do anything more to the engine. As the beast came to life, excitement and joy overwhelmed me. We had accomplished the biggest task of restoring this car.

We next had to fix the body of the car. I quickly learned three words that would stay with me forever: *Bondo, fiberglass,* and *resin.* We repaired the big holes in the car's frame with the fiberglass and resin. If you have ever worked with these two materials, you know the trials and tribulations that come in working with them. They're very messy. I guess a good example of what working with them is like is when children use glue to stick papers together. If you use too much glue, the paper becomes more difficult to work with. Well, it's kind of the same idea with fiberglass and resin. You have to work fast with them, or they become a large problem. Luckily, that was not my job. Dad decided to take on that task. I'm not sure he really trusted me with the fiberglass and resin, so he made it my task to apply Bondo to some of the dents and areas of the car that needed it. Dad warned me that the more Bondo I put on the car, the more sanding I would have to do to get it smooth enough to match the car.

After completing the bodywork, we next had to give the car a fresh coat of paint. We chose the car's original color because we thought that if we made any mistakes, it would make them harder to discern. I felt ready to take the car down the road for a test drive when Dad had one more thing he wanted me to do: place on the decals that he had ordered. As I placed on the two side decals and one rear decal, Dad looked as excited as I was.

When I took the car down the road for the first time, I couldn't help but feel that this part of the journey was complete. I'm not sure how many times I thanked Dad for helping me, but I can tell you I obviously didn't do it enough. I think that was my favorite car that I have ever owned—maybe because it was my first car, maybe because I had a lot of memories in that car. But I think that it still is my favorite car because of the bond that Dad and I forged over it. I miss that car. I miss working on that car with Dad.

# Chapter 9

# *A VERY MERRY CHRISTMAS*

As my wife, my children, and I left to visit my parents for Christmas in 2012, we all felt excited that Dad was home and looked really well. We all had faith that Dad was healed and that he would be around to watch Andrew and Elizabeth grow up.

When we arrived at my parents' home, Dad had already moved things out of the garage so we could pull in and unload the van without the weather interfering. As we emptied that van, I noticed that Dad had a lot of energy and looked full of life. You would never notice that he was battling cancer. We all hugged Mom and him, thankful that we had made the nine-hundred-mile trip without any issues. With Andrew and Elizabeth both still very young, it took us a bit longer than a day because they needed a break approximately every two hours.

After unpacking, we sat around while Andrew and Elizabeth went into the closet in my old bedroom to pull out all the toys that Mom had saved from my childhood. Every toy that my kids pulled out brought back so many memories of when I was that age. Building blocks, my wooden train, and other toys took me back to a time when life was so much simpler. I can remember playing with that train, which had some wheels missing on it. My Matchbox car collection caused a big excitement, especially for Andrew. The kitchen play set thrilled Elizabeth.

For some odd reason, even though I knew we would have a great Christmas, I felt some nervousness. Dad was doing great, and we all really felt encouraged by how well he was responding to radiation and chemotherapy treatments. Dad moved around and acted as if nothing

21

bothered him. It was a very special Christmas because my sister, Melissa, had flown in for a visit that year.

Christmas morning, I felt as if I were a child again. The only issue was that my kids had to come wake me up to open presents. Dad took pictures of the kids as they opened their gifts. It took me back again to when I was their age. Dad had done the same thing thirty years before, when Melissa and I were young children.

I remember going to Grandma and Grandpa's house for lunch and another round of presents. We lost Grandma in 2002 and Grandpa in 2011. Over the last few years, Mom and her siblings had rotated having Christmas, but because we wanted to remain on the cautious side, Mom decided to hold it at their house. It was good to see all of Mom's relatives, aunts, uncles, and cousins. Of course, all the male cousins sat around and talked about sports. All the other cousins engaged in watching the young kids play together.

As the evening wound down and Mom's relatives departed, I couldn't help but feel that this was one of the best Christmases I would ever have. It was almost perfect! We still had a couple of days left in town, so we made sure that we spent as much time with Mom, Dad, and Melissa as possible.

As we packed to head for home, I pulled out a bag of letters I had my students create for Dad. As I handed them to him, I could see tears starting to well up in his eyes. I told him that everyone in my class was pulling for him to make it through and visit our class when he was healed. As always, I started to cry because I didn't want to leave.

Before we piled into the van, Melissa's friend took a picture of our whole family. I still have that picture posted as my cover photo on Facebook. Little did I know this would be the last family photo that we ever took.

## Chapter 10

# *FINDING JESUS*

As I packed and headed off to college, I thought that I would have the best time of my life there. I was finally on my own, with no rules, no curfews, and no parents. Of course, it made me sad to move out, but I felt excited about college. I had it all planned; I would major in secondary education with a concentration in math and science. I had earned a scholarship that would help pay for part of my schooling. It so relieved Dad that I had earned a scholarship because he didn't know how else I could pay for college, outside of taking out loans. The only issue? I would soon find out that I couldn't easily use my time wisely.

I spoke with Mom and Dad every week to let them know how I was doing. Little did they realize I hadn't been attending class regularly and didn't take my studies seriously. Little did I realize that this would cause a problem. The fact was I didn't know if I wanted to stay in college at that time. I didn't want the hassle of having responsibility for that. I hated going to a few classes. I felt that none of my professors gave me the time of day to help me out. I went to a room where I could get help, especially with math, of all things. As I sat there while super-smart people tried to assist me, I wasn't sure that I would succeed. These people talked way over my head for me to learn anything.

At the end of my first semester, how poorly I had done shocked me. Everything had come to me so easily in the past that I found it hard to believe I was a student who didn't take school seriously. I had been so reliable previously that I knew this would disappoint my parents, especially Dad.

At the beginning of my second semester, my parents received an unpleasant notice in the mail. The college informed my parents that it would revoke the scholarship that I had earned. When I received a call from Dad, it surprised me. Mom was normally the one who called me. Dad informed me of the news and told me how disappointed he was I couldn't keep up with my schoolwork. I felt as if I had let everyone down and was determined to get things straightened out for my second semester.

I had been working at the chemistry lab to help pay my way through college when I met a guy named Mike Ehinger. The previous semester, Mike had talked to me about life and what I wanted to do in the future. I found Mike different from most people I had met, mainly because he was so friendly. Most other people I had met seemed closed off and didn't want to talk. I remember having dinner with Mike one Thursday night and then deciding to hang out with him. As we left dinner, we did not head back to my dorm. I asked Mike, "Where are we going?"

Mike replied, "We're going to a Chi Alpha meeting."

My brain just stopped. Chi Alpha was a campus ministry. I couldn't figure out what was going on. I knew that I needed change, but I didn't know whether I was ready for something that I didn't have control of. When I walked in, all these eyes staring at me terrified me. Most of the people came over and introduced themselves to me. And after seeing worship and listening to the Message, I knew that I was ready to make a life change. At the end of the night, I gave my life to Jesus.

I felt grateful that Mike decided to take me under his wing and nurture me over the next few months. I became part of his small group shortly after giving my life to Jesus. It was like on-the-job training. While Mike and I worked at the chemistry lab together, we would always have conversations about life, what the Holy Spirit did in our lives, and upcoming activities that we looked forward to. Mike felt like a big brother to me. He always checked in on me. We would occasionally have dinner together. We would see each other every Thursday night at our weekly worship. I truly owe a great deal of thanks to Mike. Our paths didn't cross by random chance; it was truly the work of the Holy Spirit. If God hadn't had Mike cross my path, I truly believe that I would not be here today.

I didn't know how Dad would handle this news. Mom always seemed open to different things, if they were legal. But Dad wasn't the world's most religious person. He didn't attend church that much and seemed uncomfortable whenever he went. Throughout the next few months, Dad and I didn't see eye to eye in several situations. I can remember one night, when I was home because my car wasn't working properly, Dad and I had a huge argument, after which I went to my room. I just began to pray for God to intervene in this situation. About twenty minutes later, Dad came into my room and said, "I know you've been praying." I looked up at him, a bit startled. I wasn't sure how he knew, but I think it opened my eyes to the power of the Holy Spirit.

Throughout the rest of my college career, how well I did pleasantly surprised me. I changed my major after many hours of prayer and realized that it would add an extra year to my education. In any case, I concentrated my studies in elementary education, working with younger children, as a male can have a powerful influence. I worked harder to bring my grades up. I had a bump here and there, but with support from my newfound friends and my renewed faith in God, I felt this was the change I needed.

Mom was initially skeptical but relaxed after she received more information. The support of my friends encouraged me, and I trusted God to guide my path. People saw a different side of me once I let go of the anger and disappointment I had held on to over my teenage years. From academics to relationships, everything got exposed.

As my college career went on, everything that I did seemed to work out. I did great in my studies, read the Bible every day, and continued friendships that were bonded by God's love. Little did I realize that I would meet my wife my junior year. She quickly knew that we would get married. Me—I recognized this a little slower. I put the thought in the back of my mind, but normally, when I do that, those thoughts fade away. This thought wouldn't go away. I decided that I would speak with my pastor, Steve, about this feeling.

I sat down with him one morning and explained what I thought. We agreed to pray about it for the next few weeks, and then, we would have another meeting to discuss the results of earnestly seeking God. The results: This was a path that I couldn't turn my back on.

## Chapter 11

# *THE BIG SPRING BREAK BUMMER*

I had thought spring break 2013 would be great. I could spend some time with my parents. But I had received word Dad was not doing as great as we thought. I wasn't worried, though. In my mind, Dad would get healed. Dad had sent a letter to my class to thank them for the Christmas cards and say he looked forward to meeting all of them when he and Mom came down during the summer.

Dad was still in the hospital when I got to Michigan, but I was able to help Mom bring him home when he got released. I couldn't stay long, however. I had a medical procedure scheduled for Wednesday, but I would get to spend some quality time with Dad. When we got Dad home, we had a few conversations about how he felt and how he could still do all the things he looked forward to. You see, Dad had found God a few years back. I owe that conversion to God, but an assist to Mom and Dad's pastor, Pastor Jim. He was the first of their church's pastors he could relate to. I felt so grateful that he had helped guarantee Dad's ticket to heaven.

I got ready to leave Mom and Dad's house early Tuesday morning to make it back in Jacksonville in time for my procedure. For some reason, I had an odd feeling of despair. I couldn't understand it. If I felt so sure Dad would be okay, why did this awful feeling well up in the pit of my stomach? I didn't have time to sort it out. I knew I had a twelve-hour drive ahead of me. I quickly kissed Mom and Dad goodbye and got into the car. I wish I had more time to spend with Mom and Dad, but we all led extremely busy lives.

As I pulled into my driveway, I felt tired, sore, and emotionally spent.

I couldn't think straight. I could barely move. My eyes were exhausted. I just wanted to go to bed. During the drive home, I couldn't think of anything except turning around and going back. But I finally pulled into my driveway, and I called Mom to let her know I made it home okay. I hugged my wife and kids good night and crashed into bed. I knew it wouldn't get any easier, using the rest of my spring break to recover from my medical procedure.

Mom contacted me a few days after my procedure to check whether I was okay. I told her everything looked fine, but I found out she had a hidden meaning behind her call. She told me Dad hadn't felt really well after I left, so they decided to do a scan of his body to see if he had made any progress from the chemo treatments. I could hear Mom starting to choke up in trying to get her words out.

She informed me that Dad's lung tumor had only shrunk by one millimeter. What was worse, the cancer had spread and had become more aggressive. We now had to determine if we wanted Dad to continue his treatments, or if we wanted to make the most difficult decision of our family's lives. I knew that Melissa was coming in to visit Dad, so we would have to determine the best situation for him. Mom told me that she had a meeting with some of Dad's doctors coming up to determine the best decision for our family.

I thought about all the praying and meditation that our family had done since August after finding out about Dad's condition. I wasn't sure why our prayers went unanswered. I began to become frustrated and angry. At times, I felt as if I had lost my faith in God. How could He let this happen to my family? How come He didn't bring more comfort to us? Bitterness overcame me, to the point where I thought about giving up on God. If He wouldn't heal Dad, why should I continue His path? Why should I continue having a personal relationship with Him?

People would ask me, "How is your dad doing?"

"He's doing okay," I would reply.

In reality, Dad wasn't doing very well. I wasn't doing very well. I always heard other people tell me, "I understand." In the back of my mind, I knew they really didn't know how I felt. In fact, I had convinced myself that, unless they had gone through the same situation, they didn't have any right to tell me they understood. I felt miserable, but I didn't let others around me know it. I just decided to push my feelings aside and continue to plow through, hoping that work would occupy my time.

As spring break came to an end, I knew I was going to be a wreck. The future was uncertain. What lay ahead would alter the course of my life forever.

# Chapter 12

# *WORKING NINE TO FIVE*

Amy and I got married in 2001. I was working as a teacher in a Detroit suburb, my first teaching position. Amy was working in Detroit as a teacher. For those of you who have ever worked with inner-city children, you know the trials that come with that territory. One of my first impressions at this school was that I would need to stay tough. Some of these children would never live any part of their life outside these walls.

As we dismissed students for the first day, I saw a bread truck pull up next to a grocery store across the street from the school. As the bread guy took his delivery into the store, the horrific scene that took place amazed me. Parents of our students ran over to the bread truck and grabbed loaves of bread by the handfuls. I realized that I was looking at desperate people doing anything to survive. It gave me my first real glimpse into the life of an inner-city family.

While teaching, I met a student named Dustin. Dustin was the opposite of most of the other children. He was well groomed, spoke English perfectly, and was a top-notch student. He had something different about him. I had an instant rapport with him. It's interesting whom God puts in your path. (Years later, I would learn that God had placed him in an area that needed the Holy Spirit.)

I had worked at the school for about two years when I lost my grandma. I felt that my world had come crashing down. Everyone in our family loved Grandma. She was a very gentle, giving person. This only added to the fact that I struggled to keep my head above water at school. Some of the issues that I had no control over turned me angry and bitter. It came to the point where I sought God for direction. After much prayer, I decided to resign my position at the school and take a job as a security guard at a Pfizer facility. I didn't know how Dad would take the news. I hoped that he would understand I needed to reevaluate what I wanted to do for a living. Working the midnight shift, I really had a chance to think about the path that I was taking. I felt some relief and found myself surrounded by godly people, especially my friend Phil.

The opportunity arose when I decided to try teaching again. I obtained a sixth-grade math position at a school down the street from the juvenile detention center in Detroit. Amy took a position as an eighth-grade teacher at the same school. I think that ended up being the biggest mistake of my career. Instead of seeking God for his direction, I made an unintelligent decision because I thought I needed to prove to myself that I was a good teacher. From the first day of that job, I experienced nothing but trouble. I had serious health issues, migraines and seizures. Amy had some health issues as well. Then, about three months in, I had an altercation with the principal and found out her true feelings about my wife and me. I had to leave for the last few months because my health was giving me issues.

Then, Amy discovered that teachers, under the principal's direction, were changing answers on the state assessment to inflate their scores. I realized at that point I needed to focus on God and what He wanted, instead of on myself. How far had I fallen? What if I couldn't get out of this? What would I do for a job, because I wouldn't be a security officer the rest of my life. What had I done?

After returning to work, I needed to focus on preparing for Onslow County's Relay for Life. I had worked as a committee member for the last few years. In fact, I was one of only a few people who could construct our display, so that got me out of work for a half day. In setting up early Friday afternoon, our display went up quickly. As I read the names on the board, I was honored to have Dad's name as part of the survivors' side. At the beginning of the event, a survivor lap occurs, where all those people who are beating cancer walk around the track. As the lap started, I couldn't help but visualize Dad and me walking around that track someday. I found it very inspiring to see all those people cancer had affected. I put my faith in God performing a miracle for our family that the whole world would hear about.

After spending a late night at the Relay for Life, I went home to get some sleep. I needed to get back early to help tear down the display and take all the materials over to the school to be unloaded. In the midst of tearing it down, I received a message from Mom. She said that a nurse was going to speak with her and Dad about options for helping Dad. I didn't realize at the time that Dad was in worse shape than I thought. Mom said that once they learned about Dad's in-home care, she would let me know what choices we had for helping Dad.

Dad had a hard time doing everyday tasks by that point. In fact, they had brought in a hospital bed to help him feel more comfortable. I think what most surprised me was that Dad did not communicate with other people. I believe that he tried to communicate but just could not get anything to come out of his mouth. When I heard this information, I didn't know how to handle it. I had a sick feeling in the pit of my stomach. I didn't say anything to anyone because I wanted to take in what happened around me.

When Melissa flew in to be with Mom and Dad, she couldn't communicate with Dad because he was so weak; he couldn't talk. Most of Mom's family was there. Pastor Jim was also there, talking to him, but I'm not sure Dad could understand what was going on. Mom and the rest of the family went into the kitchen, leaving Dad and Pastor Jim in the family room. After everyone left, God decided to bring Dad home.

Melissa called me shortly after Dad went to be with the Lord. After I hung up the phone, I called Amy in and let her know that Dad had just been taken to heaven. We cried together for a few minutes, and after that, Amy left the room so I could gather my thoughts.

Everything I had ever accomplished was totally worthless now. I thought about how Dad would miss the best years of his life. He would never get a chance to see and be with Andrew and Elizabeth. They would never get a chance to grow up and know Grandpa. I would never get to see Dad show his Massey-Harris tractors. I would never get to see Grandpa's relationship with Andrew blossom. Elizabeth would never get the opportunity to truly know Grandpa. How would they take the news?

I guess when you're four and two years old, life isn't so complicated. In your midthirties, life isn't so simple.

And what made things more complicated? I had just started my master's degree at East Carolina University. I know, the program was entirely online, but it added one more thing to my already emotional plate.

# Chapter 13

## *FINALLY FINDING SUCCESS*

I got an interview for a fifth-grade teaching position in the fall of 2004. After the interview, my best friend, Jeremy, and I went golfing. About halfway through my round, Amy called me to tell me that I had gotten the job! I felt so excited that I didn't care about golfing anymore. I was determined to make that the best job I had ever done.

While the first year went great, the second year took its toll on me. I prayed that God would somehow pull me through. I began to wonder if God really wanted teaching to be my occupation. After the second year, I didn't know why things were turning out the way they were. Then, at the beginning of year three, I finally determined that I was totally not at the correct school. Our principal had moved on and taken some of my good friends with him. I never liked the new person in charge, and the assistant principal only had a background in music. In fact, the new principal didn't even have an administration degree.

In an effort to boost my students' morale, I decided to hold a Thanksgiving Day feast for the students and their parents. We had done this the previous year with great success. Well, after getting clearance from the assistant principal and inviting all my students and their parents, I was told by our school's administration that I could not hold this event because it would take up too much instructional time—as if any learning would take place on the day before Thanksgiving vacation. Well, I decided to take a stand for the students and parents and protest that this feast was a great way to connect with parents. Free food—who doesn't like free food? Apparently, our administration didn't like the idea. I decided to report it to someone higher up. This didn't appease our administration. In standing up for my students, I got an ultimatum: step down, or else. I went home and prayed about my decision.

In earnestly seeking the Lord, I heard Him say, "The time to move on is now. I have better things that await you." The next day, I had made my decision. I decided to step down, but not without upsetting many students and parents with the decision. I had given three years of my life to this school, advocating for the students, only to see it destroyed by people who were not even qualified to hold positions of leadership. This was it. Now, I really had to trust in the Lord. I think that was one of only a few times that I had no choice but to trust God.

In a totally unrelated turn of events, Amy lost her job at the same time. We had no money, had just bought a house, and were trusting God to show us the way. Totally feeling dejected, I woke up one morning after Amy had gone out and found a card with my name on it. I will never forget the words inside it: "The real mark of a man is not how he celebrates victory, but what he does in the face of adversity." I was determined to get back on my feet.

At that point in our lives, I asked Amy how she felt about possibly moving out of Michigan. After much prayer, we decided to send out our resumes across the country. The first phone interview that we had was with a school district in Arizona. Moving so far away from my family didn't necessarily thrill me. After praying, I didn't feel we were supposed to go there. After talking with a few people from around the country, I had a chance to talk with some people from Jacksonville, North Carolina. After speaking and interviewing with them, something told me that we were supposed to travel to that place. It meant Amy and I could teach at the same school. We decided to meditate about it; we accepted the offer.

During Thanksgiving 2006, I moved down to Southwest Elementary, just outside Jacksonville. I won't lie; it made me feel very nervous and excited at the same time. I would have to jump right into teaching. Because of my previous teaching experience, I wouldn't get a mentor to help me along. Oh, did I mention I went from teaching middle school to teaching second grade? Uh, yeah. This was unchartered territory for me. I had to trade my brash personality for a more understanding, caring personality.

How could I pull this off? I didn't want to offend every student on my first day at my new school.

The night before I started, I had so many thoughts that they kept me up late. What would happen if I failed right out of the box? How would students take a teaching change in the middle of the year? What if the other teachers around me found me strange? Well, my first day, I found I was just as crazy as everyone around me. I guess that helped me loosen up. When I felt very productive on the first day, I breathed a sigh of relief. I wasn't a failure! I had more success in one day at this school than in my six previous years in Michigan combined.

I thought about how my university adviser and the teacher I student-taught with never thought I would make it as a teacher. I thought about my former students, who were disappointed that I had to leave because I stood up for them. I thought about my family, especially Dad, who knew that I would one day have success. I had finally arrived! The next ten years would be the most successful in my and Amy's teaching careers. Hallelujah! Someone up there loves me!

I remember seeing Dad spending a lot of time with Pastor Jim at Grandpa's one hundredth birthday party in the summer of 2010. He seemed so interested in what Pastor Jim had to say. I had never seen Dad so excited to talk about God. They say miracles happen every day. I truly never thought this one miracle would come to fruition. As I thought more and more, I realized that my prayers had finally been answered. Then, I knew that I would finally get to see Dad in heaven when our times came. I didn't realize that part of that promise would come too soon.

During our time in North Carolina, I saw a change in Dad. He seemed happier and full of life. I couldn't believe the change in him. I had missed being close to him. I kept thinking, *God must have gotten a hold of his life!* I thank God that Dad had a pastor who could relate to him.

# Chapter 14

# *THE DARKEST DAY*

As I prepared for my flight north following Dad's death, a series of events took place. First, my flight from Jacksonville to Charlotte got canceled due to fog, so I made the decision to drive (a decision that I would feel grateful for later). On my way, I ran into three different severe thunderstorms through West Virginia and Ohio. My thought? The devil is trying to stop me from going. I would not give in! My determination pulled me through.

I pulled into Mom and Dad's driveway around ten at night. My sister was there to greet me with Mom. When I walked through the kitchen and into the family room, I saw Dad's hospital bed sitting in the room. My heart sank. Again, I was the only family member who wasn't there when Dad died. (Many years earlier, this also happened when my grandpa died in the hospital.) I didn't see how I could face anyone at that point, including God. Why was He putting me through this? As I unpacked my things and crashed on the couch, I felt mad at a lot of things: mad at myself for my canceled flight, mad at myself for the weather, mad at myself for not being with my family. I would have to push those feelings away for a while. I needed to stay strong for Mom. Anger wouldn't help anything at this point.

When we arrived at the funeral home, I hung up my jacket and went into the room where Dad was. Looking down at Dad, I instantly began to regret all the bad moments we had. After thinking about that for a few moments, I began to think about all the good times Dad would miss. Dad had been getting ready to retire and start his journey to do all the things he loved doing. He would miss seeing his grandchildren grow up. He wouldn't see me earn my master's degree. He wouldn't ride his motorcycle and show his vintage Massey-Harris tractors.

I found the visitation very difficult. I saw relatives whom I hadn't seen in several years. Some of my previous teachers stopped by. I was very glad to see one of my sixth-grade teachers, Mrs. Gillingham, stop by. She was one of my favorite teachers. I was glad that my best friend, Jeremy, spent a lot of time with me at the visitation as well. Amy and my children were the only people missing. I didn't want to burden them with the emotional baggage and stress of coming with me.

I didn't sleep very well that night, even though I felt emotionally drained. The next day wouldn't be any easier. Getting dressed for the funeral, I decided to wear a black shirt, black pants, my black fedora, and my Snoopy motorcycle tie to honor Dad. To this day, whenever I wear that outfit, I think of how much fun Dad had riding his motorcycle. I had to stay strong for my family that day. It was already hard enough on Mom. I felt she didn't need me to fall apart. I thought that would just make her more upset.

On our way to the burial site, I wondered what would happen with Mom. To my surprise, Mom held up well. Because Dad served in Vietnam—a topic he rarely spoke about—we were able to have a memorial service with honors, including a twenty-one-gun salute. After the funeral, we received memorial dog tags. I wear those tags every day to honor Dad. Melissa received a set of dog tags and some bullet shells. Mom got the actual dog tags Dad wore, some bullet shells, and the American flag she displays in the room we stay in when we visit her. I had some memorial dog tags made too—one for Andrew and one for Elizabeth.

Melissa went back to California a few days after Dad's funeral. I also planned to return to North Carolina, but I decided to stay an extra week to help Mom with things she needed done. I also wanted to stay for support; that way, she wouldn't feel as empty as she would have felt if both of us left. We visited the bank and the monument store so we could select a gravestone for Dad. The rest of the week, we just sat back and relaxed, giving me time to think and recover from a very busy week.

Before I left, Mom gave me the pedal-powered Massey-Harris tractor that Dad had kept for Andrew. I loaded all my things, including the tractor, into my car. I really didn't want to leave, but I knew I really didn't have any choice. God made it possible for me to stay an extra week with Mom, because the school had put in a special request so I could collect my salary for the two weeks I was away.

As I made my way home, I couldn't help but think about Andrew and Elizabeth. When I walked through the door, they ran up to me and gave me a hug. Knowing that they would never get to hug Grandpa again made me feel sick to my stomach. As I brought the tractor into the house, I told Andrew, "Grandma thought it would be best to give you the tractor that Grandpa was saving for when you get older." He sat on the tractor and pedaled a few times. I knew that seeing his grandson using that tractor would have made Dad really happy.

The next day, I dropped by the school to let them know that I would return on Monday. I had a long talk with Vickie, the principal, about what I should expect, what feelings I might go through, and how to handle questions that students might have. I really wasn't prepared to return. In fact, I had it in the back of my mind to take a leave of absence and stay with Mom until the summer. I felt guilty leaving Mom, knowing that she was by herself. I thank God that Melissa's dog, Lady, was still there. At least she gave Mom some company.

It turned out Lady was a very special dog. Although Lady was already fourteen when Dad died, she stayed around for another four years to keep Mom company, until she decided to sell the house and move to town. Amy and I really do believe God kept Lady for an extra four years to comfort Mom in her time of need.

Chapter 15

# THE INSPIRATION

Sometimes, you just have to realize that whatever you believe doesn't compare to the things that God has in store. For example, I think back to my graduate classes at East Carolina University. I had decided to pursue a master's degree in instructional technology through a program related to Onslow County Schools because the entire program took place online. Dad had passed about four weeks into my program, and I didn't know if I wanted to continue. As I thought about what Dad would want me to do, I decided to press on and get my degree. And through that program, I met a lady named Tonya Quinn. Because of the online nature of the program, we would probably never meet face to face, but little did I know that God would connect us through similar situations.

I remember finishing an assignment and waiting for Tonya to turn in her portion of the assignment. I hadn't heard from Tonya, and I was getting nervous that we would not turn in our assignment on time. I found out later that Tonya had a great reason why it took her a long time to submit her part to me. Her mom had cancer. Finding this out, I immediately felt like a heel for being so selfish, thinking of how a late assignment would affect me. It was at that time I realized that God had placed us in the same group purposely; it didn't happen by accident. God placed me there to help Tonya through her trials with cancer.

As we opened up to each other, I felt as if I had met someone who knew what I had gone through. I felt that I could help support Tonya to carry on with her life. If you've ever had a parent get cancer, you know what I'm talking about. I'm not sure I ever felt closer to a classmate, especially to one I never met in person. When I heard that Tonya's mother had passed, I felt the same way that I did when I lost Dad. Only people like us who have endured this share such a bond. When it came time for us to graduate, thinking about Dad, Tonya's mom, and all those who have lost a parent overwhelmed me. I was happy that I had made it to the end of the road with my degree. I also felt sad that we could not share our joy with our closest loved ones.

It's really amazing who God puts in your path. After seven years at Meadow View, I transferred to Richlands Primary. I didn't know the staff very well, and I felt like a loaner out on an island. But then I met the assistant principal, Susan Agrue. As we got to know each other a little more, I found out her husband, Charlie, was battling cancer. Because I lost Dad to cancer in 2013, I felt an instant rapport with her. I knew the emotions and anxiety she felt, and I decided that I would start praying for her and Charlie. As the year went on, we had a few conversations about teaching and personal events that I had gone through. Susan was very understanding about the issues that I had experienced, and I told her a little bit about Dad.

As the year went on, our school staff got updates on how Charlie was doing and some of the issues that they needed prayer for. After my second teacher observation, Susan and I sat down to discuss what she saw and what I needed to work on in my classroom. As we finished our conversation, I heard the Lord tell me to give her money to help Charlie and her out. At first, she wouldn't accept it, but I wouldn't take no for an answer. She finally accepted the gift and thanked me. As she left the classroom, she asked me about Dad and his short journey battling cancer. I could tell Susan cared about other people, as someone who placed her future in God's hands. I remember when I lost my dog Bernie, she sent me a note of comfort during that unexpected time, knowing how important dogs are in my life.

As the school year went on, I kept in touch with her to see how Charlie was doing and to tell her to let me know if she needed anything. Every progress update that I received about Charlie was positive. This provided me with great motivation. Even though Dad was gone, Susan and Charlie's strength and faith really encouraged me. It made me glad someone was beating cancer. Cancer is such a horrible disease. I wouldn't wish it on my worst enemy.

Susan informed us the summer of 2016 that she was transferring from Richlands Primary. The good news was that she was going to Richlands Elementary. That meant we would still get a chance to keep in contact, but less often. I kept track of Charlie's health through Facebook reports that she would post. With each post, I became more encouraged. Some of the updates mentioned procedures that must have caused Charlie unimaginable pain. For him to endure these operations and still come out positive opened my eyes to a fighter who was determined to get back to 100 percent.

Today, Charlie is home and doing well. I still receive updates on his health through Facebook posts and text messages. Every update seems to get better and better with every word that I read. He has just gone through major surgery and is doing great! I still think about Dad's cancer as a devastating blow to my life. But I take comfort in knowing that people like Susan and Charlie won't give up until God completely cures Charlie of cancer and heals his body from all his operations. They don't give up just because something goes wrong. I think it makes them stronger and allows them to have more faith that God's power remains a powerful force millions of years later.

# Chapter 16

# *THINKING ABOUT THE FUTURE*

Today, I still struggle with the emotions of losing a parent. Dad was so much a part of my life and career. I always mention to Mom what I think Dad would have felt about what I have done. I remember interviewing for a technology position in the county and feeling devastated when I didn't get the job. I remember feeling as if I let Dad down. Very rarely have I gotten rejected for a job after an interview, so I thought I had failed. Mom reassured me that Dad would be proud of me and that I shouldn't think of myself as a failure.

I think about my children, who didn't get a chance to really know Grandpa. Andrew and Grandpa had a very special bond. I have several pictures of Grandpa and Andrew. One special picture has Grandpa holding Andrew when we went to the North Carolina Zoo. Andrew was three years old when Dad left for heaven. He has some memories of his grandpa, but not as many as I would like. On the other hand, Elizabeth has very few memories of Grandpa. Elizabeth was only one when Dad was taken to heaven. She remembers Grandpa through a photo album that Mom gave us to help remember him. She often asks to see the photobook so she can see who Grandpa was. I pray for my kids, who have just about all the Vacation Bible School songs memorized. I hope that they can make the choice at an early age to follow God and do the things He wants them to do.

I think about my sister, Melissa. Melissa and Dad didn't always see eye to eye, but they did share a love of animals. I still have memories of riding mules and competing in 4-H competitions. Dad always wanted to own mules, so when Melissa got older, she rode her mule in competitions.

I think that they loved doing that together more than anything. Melissa had a side to her that I did not see when we were kids. When Dad was first diagnosed with cancer, she flew in from California to be with us. Before she left to go back, she started crying because I think in her heart she knew that Dad probably wouldn't make it. As I have gotten older, I really regret not spending more time with her growing up. We are four years apart, so it was difficult to find some common ground. I think we could have been closer, but I don't think our personalities allowed us to do that. I still pray for Melissa, hoping that she finds God soon and makes Him the most important thing in her life.

I think about Dad's motivation. He didn't always show it in the kindest way, but he certainly motivated me to do my best. I think of one time when I wanted to quit college. I called home, thinking I would talk with Mom. Instead, Dad was the only one home, so I started telling him that I thought college was too hard and I wanted to quit. Dad told me that he knew that I could do it and I just had a bad day. I used that moment to finish my degree the best way I knew how: through hard work and a never-give-up attitude.

I think about how Dad changed his life around and found God a few years before he went to heaven. He always said that it impressed him how God had turned my life around. I remember hearing from Mom that he was going to a Bible study with a friend he rode motorcycles with. I felt so excited! I had prayed for him for several years, hoping God would get a hold of his life. He had finally answered my prayers! When I came home to visit one time, I walked into Dad's bathroom and saw scriptures posted on every wall. I have since taken a moment to fill my bookshelf with sticky notes of scriptures. When we went into the basement, Dad had more signs honoring God that he had made with his scroll saw. He started going to church every Sunday, paying attention to what God said through Pastor Jim. I had always prayed for Dad to find God because I wanted to see him in heaven. I didn't realize that my prayers would get answered twenty years later.

I think about Mom and how she is doing every day. I can't imagine losing your soul mate after forty-plus years of marriage. I am impressed by how she has the courage to get up every morning and live life to the fullest. My wife and I video chat every week with Mom so she can see us and the kids. I don't think we spend enough time doing it, but we stay so busy with everything going on around us, it's the only chance we get. We try to see her when we get a chance, but often, I go see her alone because of the time it takes to get there. I take the whole family during Christmas and summer vacations. I go by myself during Thanksgiving and spring break. This gives me a chance to spend time with Mom by myself. I try to do as much as I can for her, but living one thousand miles away makes some things difficult.

I think a lot about Dad at my job. Dad worked in a school system for several years. He oversaw transportation and maintenance. I still think back to that conversation I had with him in college. I have several pictures of him and our family posted in my classroom. I keep scriptures behind me all around my bookshelf to remind me that God is in control. I want him to know that I am trying my best and that I will never give up, even in the face of adversity. For every success that God provides, I can see Dad looking down on me, smiling.

I think about other people who face this same position. Cancer is not something I would want for my worst enemy. It's such a horrible disease that affects not only the individual but also the people surrounding him or her. I pray for them daily. I want them to find peace in God's plan. Do I know why cancer took Dad's life? No, and I still don't have any thoughts on why it did. This one thing I know for sure: God will use this to further His Kingdom, and many will come to know that they will only find salvation by giving their lives to Him.

I think about how this will affect my future. I know that sounds selfish, but I still seek answers from God. I think about five, ten, twenty years from now. Where will I be? What will I do? Will Andrew and Elizabeth still remember the happy moments with their grandpa? Will Mom still be going strong? What will my sister do and think? I know that I will keep Dad's spirit alive. My wife and I have pictures of him in our house to remind us of the good times we had. Only God knows what the future holds. Will I listen carefully to what He wants me to do? Or will I totally miss what God has planned for me?

# Chapter 17

# THE LETTER

I loved Dad. I think you appreciate someone more when he or she is no longer with you. I always think about the times we had, whether happy or sad. There's a movie quote that I keep close: "The best way to remember people taken from us is to never stop loving them. Buildings burn, people die, but real love is forever."

I wrote the following letter to Dad in my journal a couple of years ago in 2016 It makes me think about savoring the moment and keeping the memories alive.

...

Dear Dad,

I wanted to let you know everyone is doing fine. I recently had an interview for a technology position, but I was unable to obtain the job. I felt like I let you down, but Mom said that you would be proud of me no matter what the outcome was. It looks like I will be returning to RPS for the next school year. I like working at RPS, so it wasn't really a big deal. Amy wasn't able to get a transfer like she was hoping and has really struggled with the idea of returning to her school. I wish I could do more other than pray, but that's all we can do at this point.

Andrew just finished up his first year in school. He loved kindergarten and did an amazing job with his end-of-the-year assessments. He is playing T-ball this summer and just finished up his spring season in soccer. He has come into his own as a defender. I remember when you and Mom signed me up for T-ball. Mom still tells everyone the story about signing me up for soccer. It still always embarrasses me every time she does it. We are working with reading so he can be ready for the upcoming school year. He is growing up so fast. You would be so proud of him!

Elizabeth is doing well. She is growing up so fast! She often asks to see the pictures that Mom had put together so your grandchildren will never forget you. She has been playing soccer. I think she is going to be a great player! She has scored several goals this year. I can't wait to see her when she gets into a more competitive league. She has been working hard on reading. I think she has my personality.

I was sad to hear that Mom could not keep up with the house anymore, so she is going to sell it. I understand that the house is getting hard to take care of. I wanted a few items that you had to keep as a fond memory of you. I took the fire engine and the Mickey Mouse lunch box that were in the basement. I also took a few of your collectables from the cabinet. We also gave Andrew and Elizabeth some of the cars and trucks that you had. I bought a bookshelf and put it on my side of the bedroom with the things I wanted. I also wanted to let you know I took some of the toy tractors and put them on a shelf in our front room.

There isn't a day that goes by where I don't think of you. You were so much a part of my life that now it feels like there's an empty void. Every day I try to give my best because that's the work ethic that you installed in me. I have pictures of you at work to remind me to always give my maximum effort.

We never said it a lot, but I want you to know that I loved you very much. I know each time we had a confrontation, you just wanted what was best for me. Many times, I wouldn't listen and then I regretted not taking your advice. Now that you're gone, I miss listening to your voice talk about whatever was on your mind.

I know that you are in heaven looking down on me. I hope that you are doing well. I know that when it's my time we'll be together again. I am so glad you found God when you did! I was worried that you wouldn't find God and we would be separated for eternity. I thank God every day for that. Until we see each other in heaven, please continue to watch over me and our family. I love you, Dad!

With love from your son,
Eric

Andrew and Elizabeth with their grandpa

Grandpa with newborn Elizabeth

Grandpa and Andrew at the North Carolina Zoo

Four generations of our family (This was taken at
Great-Grandpa's one hundredth birthday.)

Our final family photo

# About the Author

Eric LeFurge is an elementary school teacher for Onslow County Schools in Jacksonville, North Carolina. Born in Seoul, Korea, he was adopted by his dad, Rusty, and his mom, Kay, when he was four months old. Eric grew up in Chelsea, Michigan, along with his sister, Melissa. After high school, he graduated from Eastern Michigan University with a Bachelor's of Science degree in elementary education. He also earned a master's degree in instructional technology from East Carolina University.

Eric is married to his college sweetheart, Amy, and they have two children, Andrew and Elizabeth. He avidly supports cancer research and participates in Relay for Life activities.

Printed in the United States
By Bookmasters